# A SPOUSE WHO PRAYS

## A Guide to Praying For
## Your Spouse and Your Marriage

Katie Warner

I take you to be my [husband/wife]. I promise to be faithful to you in good times and in bad, in sickness and in health, to love you and to honor you all the days of my life.

-Exchange of Consent-

## Dear praying spouse,

Perhaps there is no greater gift we can give our marriage and our spouse than the gift of our prayers. As husbands and wives we entered into a covenant with our spouse and with God on our wedding day, promising to nurture this sacred relationship, which is like none other in our lives.

Often we turn to frustration, disappointment, argument, hopelessness, or maybe even just forgetfulness and complacency before we turn to prayer for our marriage. Or perhaps we may pray for our spouse, but our prayer feels rote or inconsistent. Maybe none of these dispositions describe you – maybe you are already intentional, dynamic, and devout in your prayer for your spouse and your marriage and you just want to stay the course. No matter what your prayer life looks like in this regard, this journal was written for you.

*A Spouse Who Prays* can be a powerful source for good in your marriage and in your spouse's life, if you are open to the way in which the Holy Spirit wants to work through you and through your prayers. The journal will take you through praying for an increase in the theological virtues, the cardinal virtues, the fruits and gifts of the Spirit, as well as other virtues and intentions especially important in marital life, those intentions which reside deeply in the hearts of most married men and women whether or not we realize or vocalize it.

Prayer is powerful. We marvel at stories of saints who have prayed fervently for their spouses who would later experience dramatic conversions or even joint canonizations (Saints Louis and Zelie Martin, parents of St. Therese of Lisieux)! Allow this simple prayer guide to give you the motivation and tools you need to make praying for your spouse and marriage a priority this year—and always. Holy Mary and Saint Joseph, model of virtuous marriage, pray for us!

*Katie Warner*
KatieWarner.com

# How to Use **A Spouse Who Prays**

1.  Once a week (put it on your schedule!), sit down with this journal and be aware of God's presence. **Sit in silence** for a few minutes, allowing your other duties to take a back seat to the beautiful work of praying for your spouse and marriage for this brief moment in time.

2.  **Read the special intention for the week**, with accompanying Scripture, quote, or reflection, and pray for that virtue or intention listed to grow, with God's grace, in your spouse and marriage.

3.  Write down and pray about any additional, **specific intentions** that are on the forefront of your mind related to your spouse (Examples: a conflict that keeps arising, a big decision that needs to be made, an emotional struggle your spouse is experiencing, a health issue or a challenging relationship, etc.)

4.  **Continue to pray** for the special and specific intentions each day that week. Refer to this book as needed. When praying the prayer provided on the page, feel free to substitute your spouse's name to make the prayers more personal and to write your spouse's name in the blank lines (_____) you see throughout the book.

5.  At the end of the week, **offer a spiritual bouquet** for your spouse and your marriage by writing down any gifts of prayer you offered that week for the specific intentions and for the increase of the special intention provided. (Consider planning ahead by writing these prayer commitments down and then checking them off as completed.) Some examples of gifts of prayer include:
    *   Masses
    *   Rosaries, Chaplets, and Novenas
    *   Individual prayers: Our Father, Hail Mary, Glory Be, the Memorare, Angelus, or the Prayer for Your Spouse + Marriage found in this book
    *   Daily sufferings and frustrations; Daily successes and joys
    *   Fasting

This prayer guide can certainly remain a private journal. However, if you choose to gift this to your spouse, the collection of these weekly bouquets would be a beautiful, tangible offering of love to your marriage. If you do choose to gift this journal to your spouse, the following blank page provides space to write a personal note or letter.

# A PRAYER FOR YOUR SPOUSE + MARRIAGE

Heavenly Father, you created my spouse out of your overflowing love, and you hold my spouse in existence every moment of every day, because you have a plan for _____ – a plan for our marriage. Above all, that plan is to love and to be loved, to know, love, and serve you here in this life – side by side – so that we can both behold your face, and the fullness of your love and plan for us, in heaven, for eternity.

My Jesus, help me to look at my spouse with your eyes, to care for my spouse with your hands, to listen to my spouse with your ears, to love my spouse with your heart. May your grace work in and through my spouse each day to help _____ become more conformed to your will and to the person you created him/her to be. May _____ grow in virtue every day, even in little steps and small ways, inching closer to sanctity.

Holy Spirit, animate my spouse's life and actions, so that _____ may come to live not for himself/herself but for the glory of God. May _____ become more attuned to your work in his/her life. I ask you to being your peace, purpose, and faithfulness to all of my spouse's daily work, relationships, triumphs, and trials.

Blessed Mother and St. Joseph, you are the consummate model of holy marriage. Your life together was one of selflessness, heroic virtue, and incredible charity. In the ups and downs of life's inexplicable joys and deep sufferings, amidst the sometimes-monotonous tasks of daily living, you always sought to please God and to will the good of the other. Intercede for _____ and for our marriage, so that we may aspire to reflect that kind of marital fidelity.

May the Holy Trinity be praised in and through our married life. Holy Family, pray for _____ and for our marriage.

Amen.

# FAITH

>>———<<

For truly, I say to you, if you have faith as a grain of mustard seed, you will say to this mountain, `Move from here to there,' and it will move; and nothing will be impossible to you. -Matthew 17:20

Faith is to believe what you do not see; the reward of this faith is to see what you believe. - Saint Augustine

THIS WEEK'S **SPECIFIC INTENTIONS** FOR MY SPOUSE:

Lord, I ask you to hear and answer these intentions as I humbly offer you this spiritual bouquet for my spouse's growth in faith. Through your grace, allow my spouse to have a faith that stands strong amidst whatever Satan, our culture, or the pains of life throw in our direction to weaken it. Help grow in my spouse's heart a greater desire to learn about the faith, so that through constantly expanding _____'s knowledge of you, my spouse can grow in love of you, too.

MY **SPIRITUAL BOUQUET** FOR THIS WEEK:

# HOPE

For I know the plans I have for you, says the LORD, plans for welfare
and not for evil, to give you a future and a hope.
–Jeremiah 29:11

Consult not your fears but your hopes and your dreams. Think not
about your frustrations, but about your unfulfilled potential.
Concern yourself not with what you tried and failed in, but with
what it is still possible for you to do.
–Pope John XXIII

THIS WEEK'S **SPECIFIC INTENTIONS** FOR MY SPOUSE:

Lord, I ask you to hear and answer these intentions as I humbly
offer you this spiritual bouquet for my spouse's growth in hope.
Through your grace, allow _____ to hold onto the hope that
gives meaning to life and strength to push forward in adversity.
Help _____ to always embrace hope even in the darkest
moments of his/her personal life and in our marriage, recognizing
that hope ultimately directs our gaze and goals toward heaven,
where our heart's deepest desire for happiness will be fulfilled.

MY **SPIRITUAL BOUQUET** FOR THIS WEEK:

# CHARITY

So faith, hope, love abide, these three; but the greatest of these is love. –1 Corinthians 13:13

"Love to be real, it must cost—it must hurt—it must empty us of self." -Saint Teresa of Calcutta

THIS WEEK'S **SPECIFIC INTENTIONS** FOR MY SPOUSE:

Lord, I ask you to hear and answer these intentions as I humbly offer you this spiritual bouquet for my spouse's growth in charity. Through your grace, allow _____ to look to your example and the witness of your saints, who changed the world with their deep love. Allow love to radiate from our marriage in a beautifully active way, as we grow in the kind of love that doesn't count or measure, but just gives. Help _____ to always remember that he/she was made to love and to be loved, and that when our marriage falls short of perfect love, which it will, _____ can find the source of love in you, Our Savior.

MY **SPIRITUAL BOUQUET** FOR THIS WEEK:

# PRUDENCE

"I, wisdom, dwell in prudence." –Proverbs 8:12

Blessed the one...who is not anxious to speak, but who reflects prudently on what he is to say and the manner in which he is to reply. –St. Francis of Assisi

THIS WEEK'S **SPECIFIC INTENTIONS** FOR MY SPOUSE:

Lord, I ask you to hear and answer these intentions as I humbly offer you this spiritual bouquet for my spouse's growth in prudence. Through your grace, allow _____ to apply reason and practical wisdom to everyday decisions, speech, and actions—big or small— both within and outside of our marriage. Give my spouse the prudence to seek counsel as needed, use good judgment, and to be decisive when the right direction in which to move becomes clear. In our marriage, help us to be prudent with our time and our attention given to one another and to our family.

MY **SPIRITUAL BOUQUET** FOR THIS WEEK:

# JUSTICE

>)———((

When justice is done, it is a joy to the righteous, but dismay to evildoers. –Proverbs 21:15

The source of justice is not vengeance but charity.
-Saint Bridget of Sweden

THIS WEEK'S **SPECIFIC INTENTIONS** FOR MY SPOUSE:

Lord, I ask you to hear and answer these intentions as I humbly offer you this spiritual bouquet for my spouse's growth in justice. Through your grace, allow _____ to always work to maintain and restore justice in our family and in the world around him/her. Strengthen my spouse's will to remain steadfast in giving what is owed to God (like worship) and to others (like the right to life). In our marriage and family, help us to be just in our conflict resolution and in our parenting.

MY **SPIRITUAL BOUQUET** FOR THIS WEEK:

# TEMPERANCE

Do not follow your base desires, but restrain your appetites. –Sirach 18:30

Also, temper all your works with moderation, that is to say, all your abstinence, your fasting, your vigils, and your prayers, for temperance sustains your body and soul with the proper measure, lest they fail. –Saint Hildegard

THIS WEEK'S **SPECIFIC INTENTIONS** FOR MY SPOUSE:

Lord, I ask you to hear and answer these intentions as I humbly offer you this spiritual bouquet for my spouse's growth in temperance. Through your grace, allow _____ to moderate the attraction to worldly pleasure, using material things in a way that is healthy and leads to lasting, rather than fleeting, happiness. Help my spouse to combat the temptation toward instant gratification and excess. In our marriage, help us to rely on the virtue of temperance to live a balanced life – moderating our media/digital consumption, eating and drinking habits, spending trends, and our division of work and leisure time.

MY **SPIRITUAL BOUQUET** FOR THIS WEEK:

# FORTITUDE

The Lord is my strength and my song. –Psalm 118:14

The person with fortitude is one who perseveres in doing what his conscience tells him he ought to do…The strong man will at times suffer, but he stands firm; he may be driven to tears, but he will brush them aside. When difficulties come thick and fast, he does not bend before them. –Saint Josemaria Escrivá

THIS WEEK'S **SPECIFIC INTENTIONS** FOR MY SPOUSE:

Lord, I ask you to hear and answer these intentions as I humbly offer you this spiritual bouquet for my spouse's growth in fortitude. Through your grace, allow _____ to always stand firm amidst difficulties and never stray in his/her effort to pursue the good. When life, work, marriage gets difficult, let my spouse run first and speedily toward you, and not away from you. Help _____ resist temptations and strive to live a moral, courageous life. When our vocation produces suffering, give us the fortitude to move from seasons of carrying our cross to those of resurrected joy.

MY **SPIRITUAL BOUQUET** FOR THIS WEEK:

Marriage helps to **overcome** self-absorption, egoism, pursuit of one's own pleasure, and **to open oneself** to the other, to mutual aid and to **self-giving.**

*- Catechism of the Catholic Church, 1609*

# VULNERABILITY

But he said to me, "My grace is sufficient for you, for my power is made perfect in weakness." I will all the more gladly boast of my weaknesses, that the power of Christ may rest upon me. For the sake of Christ, then, I am content with weaknesses, insults, hardships, persecutions, and calamities; for when I am weak, then I am strong. – 2 Corinthians 12:9-10

To love at all is to be vulnerable. –C.S. Lewis

THIS WEEK'S **SPECIFIC INTENTIONS** FOR MY SPOUSE:

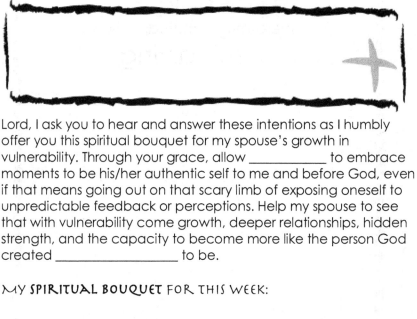

Lord, I ask you to hear and answer these intentions as I humbly offer you this spiritual bouquet for my spouse's growth in vulnerability. Through your grace, allow _____ to embrace moments to be his/her authentic self to me and before God, even if that means going out on that scary limb of exposing oneself to unpredictable feedback or perceptions. Help my spouse to see that with vulnerability come growth, deeper relationships, hidden strength, and the capacity to become more like the person God created _____ to be.

MY **SPIRITUAL BOUQUET** FOR THIS WEEK:

# PRAYER LIFE

Then you will call upon me and come and pray to me, and I will hear you. – Jeremiah 29:12

If you have lost the taste for prayer, you will regain the desire for it by returning humbly to its practice. –Pope Paul VI

Love to pray. Prayer enlarges the heart until it is capable of containing God's gift of Himself. – Saint Teresa of Calcutta

THIS WEEK'S **SPECIFIC INTENTIONS** FOR MY SPOUSE:

Lord, I ask you to hear and answer these intentions as I humbly offer you this spiritual bouquet for my spouse's prayer life. Through your grace, allow _____ to make prayer a priority every single day. Draw near to my spouse in prayer. Give _____ the fortitude to persevere in prayer in times of dryness or suffering. I pray that my spouse's prayer life is one of continual growth, which bears fruit in his/her life, in our marriage, in our family, and in the world around us. Most of all, I ask that my spouse's prayer life draw him/her closer to your Sacred Heart.

MY **SPIRITUAL BOUQUET** FOR THIS WEEK:

# SACRAMENTAL LIFE

Do this in remembrance of me. –Luke 22:19

Holy communion is the shortest and safest way to Heaven.
–Saint Pius X

So many people see the confessional as a place of defeat,
but confession is a place of victory every single time.
–Fr. Mike Schmitz

THIS WEEK'S **SPECIFIC INTENTIONS** FOR MY SPOUSE:

Lord, I ask you to hear and answer these intentions as I humbly
offer you this spiritual bouquet for my spouse's sacramental life.
Infuse _____ with your sacramental grace, and help him
develop or persevere in a habit of receiving the Holy Eucharist and
Reconciliation, so that my spouse can commune with you, be
strengthened by you, and come to you for healing. Let your
sacraments transform my spouse into the person you are calling
him/her to be.

MY **SPIRITUAL BOUQUET** FOR THIS WEEK:

# JOY

Clap your hands, all peoples! Shout to God with loud songs of joy!
–Psalm 47: 1

"Rejoice in the Lord always. I will say it again: Rejoice!"
–Philippians 4:4

Joy is a net of love by which we catch souls.
-Saint Teresa of Calcutta

THIS WEEK'S **SPECIFIC INTENTIONS** FOR MY SPOUSE:

Lord, I ask you to hear and answer these intentions as I humbly offer you this spiritual bouquet for my spouse's growth in joy. Through your grace, allow _____ to delight in his/her relationship with you, in our marriage, and in our ordinary but blessed family life. May _____'s joy be deep-rooted and contagious, becoming that "net of love" by which my spouse ignites his/her own soul and the souls of others with greater love of you. Give _____ the joy that flows first from an intimate friendship with you rather than from money, possessions, fame, or other fleeting and earthly things.

MY **SPIRITUAL BOUQUET** FOR THIS WEEK:

# PEACE

And the peace of God, which passes all understanding, will keep
your hearts and your minds in Christ Jesus.
–Philippians 4:7

Never be in a hurry; do everything quietly and in a calm spirit. Do
not lose your inner peace for anything whatsoever, even if your
whole world seems upset. - Saint Francis de Sales

THIS WEEK'S **SPECIFIC INTENTIONS** FOR MY SPOUSE:

Lord, I ask you to hear and answer these intentions as I humbly
offer you this spiritual bouquet for my spouse's growth in peace.
Through your grace, allow _____ to live a life characterized
by peace and not anxiety, handing over his/her worries to you.
Help _____ to see areas in his/her life where peace of
heart, peace within our marriage or peace within our family is
being threatened, and then have the courage to make changes
to restore your life-sustaining peace. Let our marriage also be
characterized by peace – peace in our exchanges with one
another, peace in our habits, and peace in our home environment
so as to make our home a place of refuge and a place where we
encounter Christ's own peace.

MY **SPIRITUAL BOUQUET** FOR THIS WEEK:

# PATIENCE

Be still before the LORD, and wait patiently for him.
–Psalm 37:7

Patience attains all that it strives for. He who has God finds he lacks nothing: God alone suffices. - St. Teresa of Avila

THIS WEEK'S **SPECIFIC INTENTIONS** FOR MY SPOUSE:

Lord, I ask you to hear and answer these intentions as I humbly offer you this spiritual bouquet for my spouse's growth in patience. Through your grace, allow _____ to grow in patience in small things (like waiting in traffic) and big things (like for a promotion, for growth of our family, etc.). Help my spouse to learn how to extend greater patience to others, especially within our own home, and to learn how to be patient with himself/herself and his/her own faults. Give _____ the patience that turns sinners into saints. And grant that in our marriage we grow ever better at being patient with one another.

MY **SPIRITUAL BOUQUET** FOR THIS WEEK:

# KINDNESS

[A]s servants of God we commend ourselves in every way: by purity, knowledge, forbearance, kindness, the Holy Spirit, genuine love... –2 Corinthians 6:4,6

Be the living expression of God's kindness—kindness in your face, kindness in your eyes, kindness in your smile, kindness in your warm greeting. –Saint Teresa of Calcutta

THIS WEEK'S **SPECIFIC INTENTIONS** FOR MY SPOUSE:

Lord, I ask you to hear and answer these intentions as I humbly offer you this spiritual bouquet for my spouse's growth in kindness. Through your grace, allow _____ to treat others as he/she would want to be treated (or better!) and always look for opportunities to extend a warm, loving, merciful and *kind* hand toward anyone in need, even and especially in our own home. I pray that he/she will be motivated to intentionally spread kindness at home and elsewhere in some small way, every day. Let our own marriage be characterized by kindness toward each other in both our words and actions.

MY **SPIRITUAL BOUQUET** FOR THIS WEEK:

# GOODNESS

Surely goodness and mercy shall follow me all the days of my life;
and I shall dwell in the house of the LORD forever.
–Psalm 23:6

A morally good act requires the goodness of its object, of its end,
and of its circumstances together.
–Catechism of the Catholic Church 1760

THIS WEEK'S **SPECIFIC INTENTIONS** FOR MY SPOUSE:

Lord, I ask you to hear and answer these intentions as I humbly
offer you this spiritual bouquet for my spouse's growth in goodness.
Through your grace, allow _____ to honor you by always
doing what is right. Help my spouse to avoid sin and make morally
good choices, a demonstration of his/her love for you and a
response of gratitude for *your* great goodness in our own lives.
Help _____ to look for goodness all around him/her and
then to spread goodness to others. In our marriage, give us the
grace and intention to be good to one another – even in just the
small, daily ways and acts that build a good marriage baby step
by baby step.

MY **SPIRITUAL BOUQUET** FOR THIS WEEK:

# GENEROSITY

In all things I have shown you that by so toiling one must help the weak, remembering the words of the Lord Jesus, how he said, "It is more blessed to give than to receive."
–Acts 20:35

Teach us to give and not to count the cost.
–St. Ignatius of Loyola

THIS WEEK'S **SPECIFIC INTENTIONS** FOR MY SPOUSE:

Lord, I ask you to hear and answer these intentions as I humbly offer you this spiritual bouquet for my spouse's growth in generosity. Through your grace, allow _____ to be generous with his/her time, talent, and treasure. Help _____ to see opportunities to be generous at home and outside the home. In our marriage, transform our hearts so that they may overflow with generosity toward one another, setting an example for our family as well. When we are tempted toward selfishness, help us to give generously instead, not counting the cost.

MY **SPIRITUAL BOUQUET** FOR THIS WEEK:

# SELF-CONTROL

He who keeps his mouth and his tongue keeps himself out of trouble. - Proverbs 21:23

Look toward Heaven, where Jesus Christ is waiting for you with His saints! Be faithful in his love, and fight courageously for your souls. – Saint Felicity

THIS WEEK'S **SPECIFIC INTENTIONS** FOR MY SPOUSE:

Lord, I ask you to hear and answer these intentions as I humbly offer you this spiritual bouquet for my spouse's growth in self-control. Through your grace, allow _____ to overcome temptation and deny self of things that could draw him/her away from you – even if they are good things that just require time and temperance to find their right place in my spouse's life. Allow _____ to guard his/her words, so they are used with discretion, and to monitor his/her thoughts and actions, so as to bring life to himself/herself and others.

MY **SPIRITUAL BOUQUET** FOR THIS WEEK:

Love is never something
ready-made, something
merely 'given' to man and
woman; it is always at the same
time a 'task' which they are
set. Love should be seen as
something which in a sense
never 'is' but is always
only 'becoming',
and what it becomes depends
upon the contribution of both
persons and the depth of their
commitment.

-Saint Pope John Paul II

# FAITHFULNESS

His master said to him, "Well done, good and faithful servant; you have been faithful over a little, I will set you over much; enter into the joy of your master." –Matthew 25:21

Be faithful in small things because it is in them that your strength lies. –Saint Teresa of Calcutta

THIS WEEK'S **SPECIFIC INTENTIONS** FOR MY SPOUSE:

Lord, I ask you to hear and answer these intentions as I humbly offer you this spiritual bouquet for my spouse's growth in faithfulness. Through your grace, allow _____ to have the kind of faith that leads to faithfulness, allowing him/her to live in accord with the truths of the faith. May my spouse's whole life be a testament of faithfulness to you, Lord, in our marriage help our faithfulness to you produce fruit in our fidelity to one another, physically and emotionally.

MY **SPIRITUAL BOUQUET** FOR THIS WEEK:

# GENTLENESS

But the wisdom from above is first pure, then peaceable, gentle, open to reason, full of mercy and good fruits, without uncertainty or insincerity. –James 3:17

Nothing is so strong as gentleness, nothing so gentle as real strength. –Saint Francis de Sales

THIS WEEK'S **SPECIFIC INTENTIONS** FOR MY SPOUSE:

Lord, I ask you to hear and answer these intentions as I humbly offer you this spiritual bouquet for my spouse's growth in gentleness. Through your grace, allow _____ to act calmly and politely toward others, within our family and outside the home. I pray that others may characterize _____ by his/her humility and his/her thankfulness toward you. I also ask, Lord, that you give my spouse the strength to correct and accept corrections *gently,* humbly, and lovingly. Please help us in a special way within our marriage to be gentle with one another in times of vulnerability and in times of conflict.

MY **SPIRITUAL BOUQUET** FOR THIS WEEK:

# MODESTY

Do you not know that your body is a temple of the Holy Spirit within you, which you have from God? You are not your own; you were bought with a price. So glorify God in your body.
–1 Corinthians 6:19-20

Let your modesty be a sufficient incitement, yea, an exhortation to everyone to be at peace on their merely looking at you.
–Saint Ignatius of Loyola

THIS WEEK'S **SPECIFIC INTENTIONS** FOR MY SPOUSE:

Lord, I ask you to hear and answer these intentions as I humbly offer you this spiritual bouquet for my spouse's growth in modesty. Through your grace, allow _____ to be modest in thought, word, and dress.. Allow _____ to see and embrace modesty as a practice that upholds his/her spiritual dignity as your son/daughter. Help increase in my spouse a deep respect for the human person, so modesty becomes a natural corollary of that respect.

MY **SPIRITUAL BOUQUET** FOR THIS WEEK:

# CHASTITY

For this is the will of God, your sanctification: that you abstain from unchastity. –1 Thessalonians 4:3

"Chastity is a difficult, long term matter; one must wait patiently for it to bear fruit, for the happiness of loving kindness which it must bring. But at the same time, chastity is the sure way to happiness." –Pope Saint John Paul II

THIS WEEK'S **SPECIFIC INTENTIONS** FOR MY SPOUSE:

Lord, I ask you to hear and answer these intentions as I humbly offer you this spiritual bouquet for my spouse's growth in chastity. Through your grace, allow _____ to remain chaste throughout our marital vocation. My God, you know that this virtue is attacked ferociously in our culture today. Give my spouse the resolve to exhibit chastity in dress, in the media he/she consumes, and in our marriage. Help us to achieve individually and in our marrige the "successful integration of [our] sexuality" which will lead us to unity of body and spirit (CCC 2337). As our marriage grows in the virtues of modesty and chastity, let that growth be manifested in a beautiful purity of mind, heart, and body that bears good fruit in our family.

MY **SPIRITUAL BOUQUET** FOR THIS WEEK:

# HUMILITY

Do nothing from selfishness or conceit, but in humility count others better than yourselves. –Philippians 2:3

Someone once asked St. Bernard of Clairvaux what the three most important virtues are. He famously replied, "Humility, humility and humility."

THIS WEEK'S **SPECIFIC INTENTIONS** FOR MY SPOUSE:

Lord, I ask you to hear and answer these intentions as I humbly offer you this spiritual bouquet for my spouse's growth in humility. Through your grace, allow _____ to become a truly humble son/daughter of yours, who does not seek acclaim or earthly glory, but rather seeks faithfulness to you. Help my spouse to encourage others, rather than foster a spirit of pride or competitiveness. Give _____ the humility to recognize his/her weaknesses, followed by the grace to grow in virtue. In our marriage, flood us with true humility, so that rather seeking to be right, to win arguments, or to get the last word, we seek a marriage that first *loves*, admits fault, and humbly looks for the path to holiness.

MY **SPIRITUAL BOUQUET** FOR THIS WEEK:

# EMPATHY

Rejoice with those who rejoice, weep with those who weep. –
Romans 12:15

There are two forms of intelligence. One is of the mind, the other of
the heart. In the moral sphere there can be no doubt that the
empathy of the heart is incomparably more important than the
photography of the mind. Through the mind we can know and
understand, but through the heart we can love, serve, and
change the world. –Dr. Donald DeMarco

THIS WEEK'S **SPECIFIC INTENTIONS** FOR MY SPOUSE:

Lord, I ask you to hear and answer these intentions as I humbly
offer you this spiritual bouquet for my spouse's growth in empathy.
Through your grace, allow _____ to possess great empathy,
so that by entering genuinely into other people's feelings, needs,
and sufferings, he/she can be an example of your authentic love.
Our world—and our home—is full of souls in need of empathy. Help
my spouse to fill that need. Within our marriage, help us both to
grow in empathy toward one another, so that rather than being
stuck in cycles of self-validation, we seek to patiently and tenderly
put ourselves in the other's shoes and emotional state, so as to
grow in understanding and selfless love.

MY **SPIRITUAL BOUQUET** FOR THIS WEEK:

# GRATITUDE

Give thanks in all circumstances; for this is the will of God in Christ
Jesus for you. –1 Thessalonians 5:18

No duty is more urgent than that of returning thanks.
- St. Ambrose

THIS WEEK'S **SPECIFIC INTENTIONS** FOR MY SPOUSE:

Lord, I ask you to hear and answer these intentions as I humbly
offer you this spiritual bouquet for my spouse's growth in gratitude.
Through your grace, allow _____ to grow ever more
appreciative of the blessings and gifts you have given him/her.
May my spouse always offer prayers and words of thanksgiving to
you and express gratitude to others. I pray that my spouse counts
blessings more than complaints, and, especially within our
marriage, that we may look for opportunities to find and express
gratitude for our relationship with one another and for all of the
little and large ways in which we bless each other's lives.

MY **SPIRITUAL BOUQUET** FOR THIS WEEK:

SOME OF THE **MANY** THINGS ABOUT **MY SPOUSE** FOR WHICH I AM **GRATEFUL:**

# TRUST

Trust in the LORD with all your heart…-Proverbs 3:5

If your trust is great, then My generosity will be without limit.
–Jesus to Saint Faustina

THIS WEEK'S **SPECIFIC INTENTIONS** FOR MY SPOUSE:

Lord, I ask you to hear and answer these intentions as I humbly offer you this spiritual bouquet for my spouse's growth in trust. Through your grace, allow _____ to trust in your plan for him/her and for our marriage, no matter what life throws our way. May my spouse never lose hope in your ability to care for him/her. I pray that my spouse will learn how to abandon himself/herself more fully to your will and overcome any fear of the future. Grow the virtue of trust within our marriage. May we see one another as the greatest confidants and friends, counseling one another, encouraging one another, being vulnerable with one another, and calling each other to greater trust in times when trusting is hard to do.

MY **SPIRITUAL BOUQUET** FOR THIS WEEK:

# FORGIVENESS

Put on then, as God's chosen ones, holy and beloved, compassion, kindness, lowliness, meekness, and patience, forbearing one another and, if one has a complaint against another, forgiving each other; as the Lord has forgiven you, so you also must forgive. –Colossians 3:12-13

He who knows how to forgive prepares for himself many graces from God. As often as I look upon the cross, so often will I forgive with all my heart. -Saint Faustina

THIS WEEK'S **SPECIFIC INTENTIONS** FOR MY SPOUSE:

Lord, I ask you to hear and answer these intentions as I humbly offer you this spiritual bouquet for my spouse's growth in forgiveness. Through your grace, allow _____ to forgive more than "seventy times seven" times, as I know much of that forgiveness will be poured out upon me! I ask that you help my spouse to release grudges from the recent and distant past, as well as to relinquish desires for revenge, even in the hardest of circumstances, so as to experience the freedom that forgiveness brings. Within our marriage, give us the tremendous grace to forgive often, swiftly, with gentleness and humility.

MY **SPIRITUAL BOUQUET** FOR THIS WEEK:

# WORK

Commit your work to the LORD, and your plans will be established.
-Proverbs 16:3

The sanctification of ordinary work is, as it were, the hinge of true spirituality for people who, like us, have decided to come close to God while being at the same time fully involved in temporal affairs." – Saint Josemaria Escriva

THIS WEEK'S **SPECIFIC INTENTIONS** FOR MY SPOUSE:

Lord, I ask you to hear and answer these intentions as I humbly offer you this spiritual bouquet for my spouse's work life. Whether it be work at school, in the home, or in a professional environment, allow my spouse to offer his/her labor to you, Lord, seeing the good that comes from meaningful work. Through your grace, allow _____to channel the gifts and charisms you have given him/her to do his/her work well. May my spouse find fulfillment in his/her work, and positively impact others in his/her work setting. May we as spouses support one another in each other's work, while also making sure that work resides within its proper place in our relationship and lives, after God and family, and in proper proportion to rest and leisure.

MY **SPIRITUAL BOUQUET** FOR THIS WEEK:

# HEALTH & SAFETY

》》————《《

Beloved, I pray that all may go well with you and that you
may be in health; I know that it is well with your soul.
–3 John 1:2

THIS WEEK'S **SPECIFIC INTENTIONS** FOR MY SPOUSE:

Lord, I ask you to hear and answer these intentions as I humbly
offer you this spiritual bouquet for my spouse's health and safety.
God, this world can be scary and cruel, and sometimes innocent
people experience violence and pain that we can only pray they
might never endure. I ask that, through your mercy, you protect
_____ from serious illness and harm. Should my spouse
experience pain or be in a dangerous situation, send your host of
angels to be with _____, and give him/her the grace to
endure any ailment. Also flood our marriage with the strength to
fight battles of illness or other sufferings side by side, with grace
and hope.

MY **SPIRITUAL BOUQUET** FOR THIS WEEK:

# WISDOM

To get wisdom is better than gold… - Proverbs 16:16

Dost thou hold wisdom to be anything other than truth, wherein we behold and embrace the supreme good? –St. Augustine

THIS WEEK'S **SPECIFIC INTENTIONS** FOR MY SPOUSE:

Lord, I ask you to hear and answer these intentions as I humbly offer you this spiritual bouquet for my spouse's growth in wisdom. Through your grace, allow _____ to grow in this highest gift of the Holy Spirit, by which my spouse will come to value the things we believe by faith. Help _____ to have the wisdom to live a holy life and value created things because of you who created them. I pray that my spouse will share this ever-deepening wisdom with others, too, especially those within our own family, so that others and we may come to embrace and love all of the truths of the Christian faith as well.

MY **SPIRITUAL BOUQUET** FOR THIS WEEK:

# UNDERSTANDING

[W]e look not to the things that are seen but to the things that are unseen; for the things that are seen are transient, but the things that are unseen are eternal.
–2 Corinthians 4:18

Understanding is the reward of faith. Therefore, seek not to understand that you may believe, but believe that you may understand. –Saint Augustine

THIS WEEK'S **SPECIFIC INTENTIONS** FOR MY SPOUSE:

Lord, I ask you to hear and answer these intentions as I humbly offer you this spiritual bouquet for my spouse's growth in the Holy Spirit's gift of understanding. Through your grace, allow _____ to grasp, in some incomplete but beautiful way, the essence of your truth and the truths of the Catholic faith, so my spouse can possess an unwavering conviction about what we believe.

MY **SPIRITUAL BOUQUET** FOR THIS WEEK:

# COUNSEL

The wisdom of a prudent man is to discern his way, but the folly of fools is deceiving. –Proverbs 14:8

"Think well. Speak well. Do well. These three things, through the mercy of God, will make a man go to Heaven."
–Saint Camillus de Lelli

THIS WEEK'S **SPECIFIC INTENTIONS** FOR MY SPOUSE:

Lord, I ask you to hear and answer these intentions as I humbly offer you this spiritual bouquet for my spouse's growth in the gift of counsel. Through your grace, allow _____to judge how best to act in any situation, calling on the Holy Spirit's guidance. I pray that my spouse will defend the truths of the faith, living according to them as a faithful disciple of yours. May his/her good counsel serve also as a witness to our family and be of help to our marriage, so that we may inspire one another and others outside of our home to also act prudently.

MY **SPIRITUAL BOUQUET** FOR THIS WEEK:

# KNOWLEDGE

An intelligent mind acquires knowledge, and the ear of the wise seeks knowledge. - Proverbs 18:15

We can't have full knowledge all at once. We must start by believing; then afterwards we may be led on to master the evidence for ourselves. –Saint Thomas Aquinas

THIS WEEK'S **SPECIFIC INTENTIONS** FOR MY SPOUSE:

Lord, I ask you to hear and answer these intentions as I humbly offer you this spiritual bouquet for my spouse's growth in the gift of knowledge. Through your grace, allow _____to have the ability to judge things according to the truths of the Catholic faith, and see circumstances in his/her life as you see them. With this knowledge, may he also recognize your purpose for his/her life and for our marriage and family, so that my spouse may be a strong spiritual leader within our home.

MY **SPIRITUAL BOUQUET** FOR THIS WEEK:

# PIETY

Not every one who says to me, `Lord, Lord,' shall enter the kingdom of heaven, but he who does the will of my Father who is in heaven. –Matthew 7:21

[Piety] indicates our belonging to God, our deep bond with him, a relationship that gives meaning to our whole life and keeps us resolute, in communion with him, even during the most difficult and troubled moments. –Pope Francis

THIS WEEK'S **SPECIFIC INTENTIONS** FOR MY SPOUSE:

Lord, I ask you to hear and answer these intentions as I humbly offer you this spiritual bouquet for my spouse's growth in the gift of piety. Through your grace, instill in _____ a burning desire to worship you and to serve you with his/her whole self and life. I pray that this worship and service stem not from merely a sense of duty, but out of immense love for you. In those times when my spouse struggles with piety, fill him/her with a sense of your presence, grace, and love to draw them closer to your Sacred Heart.

MY **SPIRITUAL BOUQUET** FOR THIS WEEK:

# FEAR OF THE LORD

Fear God, and keep his commandments; for this is the whole duty of man. –Ecclesiastes 12:13

For the absence of the fear of God is arrogance and pride. How dare sinners sashay up to God as a chum without first falling down in repentance and fear and calling on the Blood of Christ to save us? –Dr. Peter Kreeft

THIS WEEK'S **SPECIFIC INTENTIONS** FOR MY SPOUSE:

Lord, I ask you to hear and answer these intentions as I humbly offer you this spiritual bouquet for my spouse's growth in the gift of piety. Through your grace, instill in _____ a desire never to offend you, either in word or deed, and the confidence that you will give them the grace to make this possible. Fill my spouse with awe and wonder of you, which allows him/her to respect you out of deep love. Give us a God-fearing marriage.

MY **SPIRITUAL BOUQUET** FOR THIS WEEK:

When the glamour
wears off,
or merely works a bit thin,
they [the spouses] think they

have made a mistake,
and that the real soul-mate is still
to find....

But the

"real soul-mate" is the
one
you are actually
married to.

-J.R.R. Tolkien

# DEVOTION TO MARY, THE ANGELS & SAINTS

[F]or he has regarded the low estate of his handmaiden. For behold, henceforth all generations will call me blessed. –Luke 1:48

In this way is he [the true Christian] always pure for prayer. He also prays in the society of angels… he is never out of their holy keeping. –Clement of Alexandria

THIS WEEK'S **SPECIFIC INTENTIONS** FOR MY SPOUSE:

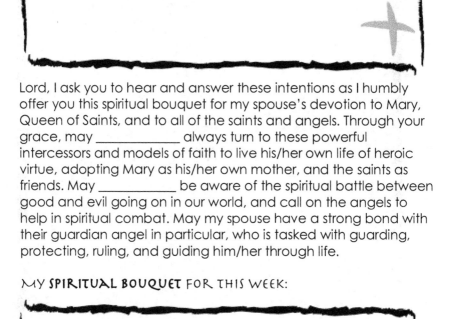

Lord, I ask you to hear and answer these intentions as I humbly offer you this spiritual bouquet for my spouse's devotion to Mary, Queen of Saints, and to all of the saints and angels. Through your grace, may _____ always turn to these powerful intercessors and models of faith to live his/her own life of heroic virtue, adopting Mary as his/her own mother, and the saints as friends. May _____ be aware of the spiritual battle between good and evil going on in our world, and call on the angels to help in spiritual combat. May my spouse have a strong bond with their guardian angel in particular, who is tasked with guarding, protecting, ruling, and guiding him/her through life.

MY **SPIRITUAL BOUQUET** FOR THIS WEEK:

# ZEAL

Never flag in zeal, be aglow with the Spirit, serve the Lord.
–Romans 12:11

Zeal reveals to us all the difference between a world grown merely
secular and old, and the youthfulness of Christian love.
–Anthony Esolen

THIS WEEK'S **SPECIFIC INTENTIONS** FOR MY SPOUSE:

Lord, I ask you to hear and answer these intentions as I humbly
offer you this spiritual bouquet for my spouse's growth in zeal.
Through your grace, give _____ a strong, action-
oriented desire to advance in the spiritual life and move in
the direction of righteousness. Provide my spouse with the
diligence to put love into action and to strengthen
resolutions to progress in virtue and holiness, making the
spiritual life a priority, even when other things threaten to
monopolize time or attention. Help us to have a relationship
full of the kind of zeal that turns ordinary marriages into
extraordinary ones.

MY **SPIRITUAL BOUQUET** FOR THIS WEEK:

# OBEDIENCE

You shall therefore love the LORD your God, and keep his charge, his statutes, his ordinances, and his commandments always. – Deuteronomy 11:1

God is more pleased to behold the lowest degree of obedience, for His sake, than all other good works which you can possibly offer to Him. -Saint John of the Cross

THIS WEEK'S **SPECIFIC INTENTIONS** FOR MY SPOUSE:

Lord, I ask you to hear and answer these intentions as I humbly offer you this spiritual bouquet for my spouse's growth in obedience. Through your grace, allow _____ to model obedience as a beautiful virtue, within our family and to those who are swayed by cultural attempts to make obedience seem unnecessary or burdensome. Help cultivate in _____ a desire to be obedient to God, His will and His laws, obedient to His Church.

MY **SPIRITUAL BOUQUET** FOR THIS WEEK:

# FAMILY

Therefore a man leaves his father and his mother and cleaves to his wife, and they become one flesh. –Genesis 2:24

Living together is an art, a patient, beautiful, fascinating journey. It does not end once you have won each other's love... Rather, it is precisely there where it begins!
–Pope Francis

THIS WEEK'S **SPECIFIC INTENTIONS** FOR MY SPOUSE:

Lord, I ask you to hear and answer these intentions as I humbly offer you this spiritual bouquet for relationships within our family. Through your grace, allow our family ties to be strong, and for peace and harmony to be present among siblings, between parents and children, within our marriage, and among our extended family. I pray that we can work to build a foundation of love and enjoyment of one another that lasts for decades, and becomes an example of intentional, self-giving family life lived well. May we prioritize relationship building and renewing activities, work to restore hurting or broken relationships within the family, and model ourselves after the Holy Family.

MY **SPIRITUAL BOUQUET** FOR THIS WEEK:

# FRIENDSHIPS

There are friends who pretend to be friends, but there is a friend
who sticks closer than a brother.
–Proverbs 18:24

There is nothing on this earth more to be prized than true
friendship. –Saint Thomas Aquinas

THIS WEEK'S **SPECIFIC INTENTIONS** FOR MY SPOUSE:

Lord, I ask you to hear and answer these intentions as I humbly
offer you this spiritual bouquet for my spouse's friendships. A good
friend is truly a treasure and can have great impact on one's life
and walk with God. Through your grace, lead my spouse toward
friends with whom they can grow in virtue, share joys and sorrows,
and festivity! I pray _____'s friends encourage him/her to
become more like the person you created my spouse to be, and
also that _____ encourages his/her own friends to grow
in holiness, both by word and example. Help us, as spouses, to
grow in friendship over time and always be the best of friends.

MY **SPIRITUAL BOUQUET** FOR THIS WEEK:

# MEEKNESS

Put on then, as God's chosen ones, holy and beloved, compassion, kindness, lowliness, meekness, and patience, forbearing one another and, if one has a complaint against another, forgiving each other; as the Lord has forgiven you, so you also must forgive. –Colossians 3:12-13

Nothing is more powerful than meekness. For as fire is extinguished by water, so a mind inflated by anger is subdued by meekness. –Saint John Chrysostom

THIS WEEK'S **SPECIFIC INTENTIONS** FOR MY SPOUSE:

Lord, I ask you to hear and answer these intentions as I humbly offer you this spiritual bouquet for my spouse's growth in meekness. Through your grace, allow _____ to become very good at moderating anger and controlling resentment toward others, finding strength through relinquishing control over to God. I pray that in situations that provoke my spouse to anger or un-forgiveness, _____ instead keeps his/her sense of peace in adversity. Help us to show meekness to one another in our marriage, because meekness is not weakness, but a manifestation of loving strength.

MY **SPIRITUAL BOUQUET** FOR THIS WEEK:

# SOLICITUDE

Love one another with brotherly affection; outdo one another in showing honor. –Romans 12:10

What is the mark of love for your neighbor? Not to seek what is for your own benefit, but what is for the benefit of the one loved, both in body and in soul. –St. Basil

THIS WEEK'S **SPECIFIC INTENTIONS** FOR MY SPOUSE:

Lord, I ask you to hear and answer these intentions as I humbly offer you this spiritual bouquet for my spouse's growth in solicitude. Through your grace, allow _____ to exhibit great "brotherly love," by demonstrating care and concern for the wellbeing of those around him/her. Rather than being envious, I pray that my spouse will admire the skills and accomplishments of others, and excel at congratulating and encouraging the people you place in his/her path. Help us show this kind of solicitude, first and foremost, to one another.

MY **SPIRITUAL BOUQUET** FOR THIS WEEK:

Love is

# patient and kind;

love is not jealous or boastful;
it is not arrogant or rude. Love

## does not insist on its

## own way; it is not irritable

or resentful;
it does not rejoice at wrong, but

## rejoices in the right.

Love bears all things, believes all

things, **hopes** all things,

**endures** all things.


-1 Corinthians 13:4-7

# CONFLICT

Love one another with brotherly affection; outdo one another in showing honor. –Romans 12:10

Marriage is a duel to the death, which no man of honor should decline. -G.K. Chesterton

THIS WEEK'S **SPECIFIC INTENTIONS** FOR MY SPOUSE:

Lord, I ask you to hear and answer these intentions as I humbly offer you this spiritual bouquet for our times of marital conflict. Conflict in relationships is a natural part of the human condition, and often manifests itself most strongly in marriage – the most intimate human relationship we share. I lift up to you, Lord, all of the trouble spots in our marriage, the conflicts and sensitivities, the arguments and vices, tendencies and cycles that are most divisive to us and ask that through your grace, you help us to transform unhealthy conflict into transformative, constructive conflict. Help us to stand side-by-side, working as a team to fight a problem, rather than seeing one another as the problem. When an opportunity for conflict arises, help us to be a stronger couple on the other side of it and to grow in love and understanding. Let us not be afraid to seek outside help from marriage-friendly counselors when needed.

MY **SPIRITUAL BOUQUET** FOR THIS WEEK:

# LEISURE

Come to me, all who labor and are heavy-laden, and I will give you rest. –Matthew 11:28

Leisure is only possible when we are at one with ourselves. We tend to overwork as a means of self-escape, as a way of trying to justify our existence. –Josef Pieper

THIS WEEK'S **SPECIFIC INTENTIONS** FOR MY SPOUSE:

Lord, I ask you to hear and answer these intentions as I humbly offer you this spiritual bouquet for my spouse's leisure. Through your grace, allow _____ to be restful and embrace leisure, avoiding the "workaholism" prevalent in our day so as to maximize time spent with you, with family and friends, and doing leisurely things that my spouse loves to do. In a culture where sometimes the art of hobbies is lost, help _____ to find ways to truly enjoy the good, the true, and the beautiful in creative, life-giving ways, seeking respite in leisure and festivity after a hard day or week's work.

MY **SPIRITUAL BOUQUET** FOR THIS WEEK:

# HONORING THE LORD'S DAY

Remember the sabbath day, to keep it holy.
Six days you shall labor, and do all your work; but the seventh day
is a sabbath to the LORD your God;...for in six days the LORD
made heaven and earth... and rested the seventh day; therefore
the LORD blessed the sabbath day and hallowed it.
–Exodus 20:8-11

Repose, leisure, peace, belong among the elements of happiness.
If we have not escaped from harried rush, from mad pursuit, from
unrest, from the necessity of care, we are not happy. –Josef Pieper

THIS WEEK'S **SPECIFIC INTENTIONS** FOR MY SPOUSE:

Lord, I ask you to hear and answer these intentions as I humbly
offer you this spiritual bouquet for our family's effort to honor the
Lord's day in our home. Through your grace, allow
_____ to be intentional – with my cooperation – in
keeping Sunday a day of rest, worship, play, relaxation, and leisure
with you and with loved ones. Our culture tempts us to work on
Sundays; let us instead protect Sundays with great determination.

MY **SPIRITUAL BOUQUET** FOR THIS WEEK:

# SELF-AWARENESS

Examine yourselves, to see whether you are holding to your faith.
Test yourselves. Do you not realize that Jesus Christ is in you? -
unless indeed you fail to meet the test!
–2 Corinthians 13:5

Know thyself, and thy faults, and thus live." —St. Augustine

THIS WEEK'S **SPECIFIC INTENTIONS** FOR MY SPOUSE:

Lord, I ask you to hear and answer these intentions as I humbly
offer you this spiritual bouquet for my spouse's growth in self-
awareness. Through your grace, allow _____ to aspire to
self-improvement, being aware of his/her faults and actively
seeking to uproot them and grow in holiness. Enlighten my
spouse's mind and heart to recognize when he/she is growing
farther away from, rather than closer to, you. Also, help
_____to be aware of his/her virtues and talents,
rejoicing in them as gifts that come from you, and exercising them
for your glory.

MY **SPIRITUAL BOUQUET** FOR THIS WEEK:

# DISCERNMENT

For God is not a God of confusion but of peace.
—1 Corinthians 14:33

Discernment itself should not be a stiff, brittle, anxious thing, but—
since it too is part of God's will for our lives—loving and joyful and
peace-filled, more like a game than a war, more like writing love
letters than taking final exams. –Dr. Peter Kreeft

THIS WEEK'S **SPECIFIC INTENTIONS** FOR MY SPOUSE:

Lord, I ask you to hear and answer these intentions as I humbly
offer you this spiritual bouquet for my spouse's discernment and
discernment within our marriage. There are so many opportunities
for discernment that life presents to us: decisions to be made
about careers, job changes, schooling, moves, friendships,
financial plans, family size, vacations, health choices…the list of
big and little discernments goes on and on. Rather than getting
overwhelmed or paralyzed by the discernment process, give
_____ the grace of a gentle heart and a firm head in
discerning your will. May we as a married couple put love of you
first, consult you in prayer, and then without fear do what we
believe is best given the circumstances, looking for peace in our
decision and trusting in you to take care of us.

MY **SPIRITUAL BOUQUET** FOR THIS WEEK:

# EVANGELIZATION

For if I preach the gospel, that gives me no ground for boasting. For necessity is laid upon me. Woe to me if I do not preach the gospel! –1 Corinthians 9:16

Every Christian is challenged, here and now, to be actively engaged in evangelization; indeed, anyone who has truly experienced God's saving love does not need much time or lengthy training to go out and proclaim that love.
–Pope Francis

THIS WEEK'S **SPECIFIC INTENTIONS** FOR MY SPOUSE:

Lord, I ask you to hear and answer these intentions as I humbly offer you this spiritual bouquet for my spouse's participation in the Church's mission of evangelization. Through your grace, allow _____ to be fervent in the mission of evangelization, in which we are all called to participate at baptism. May my spouse be filled with the love of Jesus and great joy in the Gospel, and may that inward conviction be outwardly and passionately shared with others. I pray that _____ will have the courage to share the faith with others, even when it's difficult or unpopular to do so and that our marriage will evangelize our culture, which often devalues marriage as God intended it to be.

MY **SPIRITUAL BOUQUET** FOR THIS WEEK:

# MEANINGFUL SUFFERING

I consider that the sufferings of this present time are not worth
comparing with the glory that is to be revealed to us.
–Romans 8:18

If God sends you many sufferings, it is a sign that He has great
plans for you and certainly wants to make you a saint.
–Saint Ignatius Loyola

THIS WEEK'S **SPECIFIC INTENTIONS** FOR MY SPOUSE:

Lord, I ask you to hear and answer these intentions as I humbly
offer you this spiritual bouquet for my spouse to suffer with dignity.
Though I never want to see my spouse suffer, infuse
_____ with grace in moments of suffering, allowing my
spouse to see the redemptive power in them. I pray that
_____ will offer up pain and unite sufferings with yours on
the cross, never thinking that suffering is meaningless, but rather is
an indescribably purposeful part of the Christian life – a mystery
that may not be fully understood until heaven.

MY **SPIRITUAL BOUQUET** FOR THIS WEEK:

It takes three to make love,

not two: you, your

spouse, and God.

Without God people only succeed in
bringing out the worst in one another.
Lovers who have nothing else to do but
love each other soon find there is

nothing else. Without a central

loyalty life is unfinished.

-Blessed Fulton Sheen

# MARITAL ACT

Love one another as I have loved you. –John 15:12

The spouses seal their love and commitment through their sexual union. Many today find it difficult to understand how profound and meaningful this union is, how it embodies these promises of marriage. Our culture often presents sex as merely recreational, not as a deeply personal or even important encounter between spouses.... God's plan for married life and love is far richer and more fulfilling. Here sexuality is the source of a joy and pleasure that helps the spouses give themselves to each other completely and for their entire lives.
–"Married Love and the Gift of Life," USCCB

THIS WEEK'S **SPECIFIC INTENTIONS** FOR MY SPOUSE:

Lord, I ask you to hear and answer these intentions as I humbly offer you this spiritual bouquet for our marital intimacy. Pope Saint John Paul II, in his teaching on the Theology of the Body, beautifully reminded spouses of the sexual act as one in which married persons give themselves wholly to each other, in body and spirit. Help us to love one another with a profoundly selfless love that mirrors the outpouring of self-giving love within your Holy Trinity. May we never take for granted this sacred act, which mirrors your own holy union.

MY **SPIRITUAL BOUQUET** FOR THIS WEEK:

# OPENNESS TO LIFE

And God blessed them, and God said to them, "Be fruitful and multiply, and fill the earth and subdue it." –Genesis 1:28

By its very nature the institution of marriage and married love is ordered to the procreation and education of the offspring and it is in them that it finds its crowning glory. –Gaudium et Spes, 48

THIS WEEK'S **SPECIFIC INTENTIONS** FOR MY SPOUSE:

Lord, I ask you to hear and answer these intentions as I humbly offer you this spiritual bouquet for openness to life in our marriage. We know that both the pleasurable, bonding aspect and the procreative aspect of the sexual act is innately good; help us to never sever the two gifts of the marital union by selfishness or fear. Give us the grace, Lord, to grow our family naturally, according to your will, and in times when we are unable to conceive - for whatever the reason - the grace of patience, acceptance, and hope. May we never forget that children are ultimately gifts, and not a right; give us the grace to always seek to glorify you in our family life.

MY **SPIRITUAL BOUQUET** FOR THIS WEEK:

# VOCATION

I, therefore, a prisoner of the Lord, beg you to lead a life worthy of the calling to which you have been called. –Ephesians 4:1

"The best thing for us is not what we consider best, but what the Lord wants of us," St. Josephine Bakhita

THIS WEEK'S **SPECIFIC INTENTIONS** FOR MY SPOUSE:

Lord, I ask you to hear and answer these intentions as I humbly offer you this spiritual bouquet for vocation to marriage and the other unique callings you have called us to. By your grace, allow each of us to live out our vocation to marriage with respect and with great love, since love is our first and primary vocation. In our other roles as parents, siblings, daughters and sons, our vocational careers – infuse us with your virtues to live out these callings well, seeking first to know, love, and serve you through the vocation to which you have called us. Give us a firm resolve to help one another live out our vocation with prayer, passion, and purpose.

MY **SPIRITUAL BOUQUET** FOR THIS WEEK:

# SANCTITY

You, therefore, must be perfect, as your heavenly Father is perfect.
–Matthew 5:48

Life holds only one tragedy: not to have been a saint.
–Léon Bloy

THIS WEEK'S **SPECIFIC INTENTIONS** FOR MY SPOUSE:

Lord, I ask you to hear and answer these intentions as I humbly offer you this spiritual bouquet for my spouse's sanctity. More than any other prayer intention, Lord, I implore you to mold my spouse into a great saint. May _____ come to see that you are calling him/her to the heights of holiness right in the midst of our ordinary family life. Help my spouse to see small ways to grow in sanctity every day and be fervent in taking those little steps to draw closer to you and become more like you, so _____ may spend eternity with you in the company of your saints.

MY **SPIRITUAL BOUQUET** FOR THIS WEEK:

Be subject to one another out of reverence

for Christ. Wives, be subject to your husbands

as to the Lord. For the husband is the head
of the wife as Christ is the head
of the church, his body, and is himself its Savior...

Husbands, love your wives as Christ loved the church

and gave himself up for her.

--Ephesians 5:21-23, 25


**Thank you,** my fellow prayer warriors, for joining me in praying for our spouses and marriages. May you always turn to prayer as a source of healing, a wellspring of grace, and a fountain of hope for your spouse and married life.


I would be immensely grateful if you would recommend this prayer journal to others, including the marriage ministries at your parish and diocese. Please share your feedback with me, too, or contact me for bulk discount quotes on this journal and others at:

**CatholicKatieOnline@gmail.com**

You can also find me and other great resources to raise faith-filled families at **KatieWarner.com,** on Facebook at Facebook.com/ CatholicKatieOnline, and on Instagram @katiewarnercatholic.

AMDG!

KATIE